Let Me Protect You

Let Me Protect You

POETIC BIBLE TRUTHS ABOUT EVIL

ERIC ZACK

RESOURCE *Publications* · Eugene, Oregon

LET ME PROTECT YOU
Poetic Bible Truths About Evil

Resource Publications
An Imprint of Wipf and Stock Publishers
199 W. 8th Ave., Suite 3
Eugene, OR 97401

www.wipfandstock.com

PAPERBACK ISBN: 979-8-3852-3355-7
HARDCOVER ISBN: 979-8-3852-3356-4
EBOOK ISBN: 979-8-3852-3357-1

12/10/24

Contents

Preface   *vii*

Introduction   *xi*

Rebellion

Staring into Temptation's Eyes   2

Fear the LORD   3

You Will Reap What You Sow   6

What Makes God Sad   8

For Those Who Abandon God, Eventually He Will Abandon
Them   10

Worse Than Before   12

Blasphemous   15

Can't Break Free   18

Promiscuity   20

Science???   22

Blatant Disobeying   24

Pride

The Tower of Babel   29

Blinded   32

Skeptical   34

Satan

Roaring Lion   38

I Faced the Devil   40

Questions for God   43

An Angel of Light in Disguise   46

Love of the Truth vs. The Deception of the Devil   48

Disease

Enduring Grief   52

Fight   54

You Are What You Breathe   56

Help   59

Death

Not Wanting to Let Go   64

Our Future Companion   65

tree shedding   66

By My Side   68

I Miss You   69

Death's a Doorway   72

Quietly Leaving   74

Soon a Memory   75

Answer the Door   78

Headstone   80

He Salutes You   82

Deathbed   84

Falling Asleep   86

The Kindest Words   88

Hell

The Scariest Words   92

Infernum (Hell)   94

About the Author   96

Preface

Welcome to my private collection of Christian poetry spanning five total volumes and 173 original, unique poems that I have written over the past thirty years of my life. Each volume deals with key aspects of Christianity and Holy Bible truths that have been revealed to me during my personal struggles. I have organized each one of these into an easy-to-read-and-follow format. Certain lines and stanzas in each of these poems will also have specific Bible verses referenced if you prefer to investigate further, meditate, or dive deeper into the Word.

Volume 1 focuses on God, the Bible, and surrendering. Volume 2 describes Jesus Christ and the need to be born again. Volume 3 highlights important Christian tenants that support living life to its fullest, such as grace, faith, choice, prayer, life, and blessings. Volume 4 depicts evil such as rebellion, pride, Satan, disease, death, and hell. And finally, volume 5 completes my collection with living for the future by applying Christian beliefs and putting this lifestyle into practice in serving others. It covers topics such as the Church, correction, redemption, finding purpose, the rapture, heaven, and the end of times.

I have generally written these poems whenever I had ideas or inspirations come to me and when I had the time to process them, sit down, and compose them (preferably in an uninterrupted manner). Although their actual chronological order has been lost, I feel that there is great benefit in how these poems have been organized for your understanding and reading pleasure. My brain seems to work in this manner by compartmentalizing related topics together. My intention was to document many of my own personal experiences along with my spiritual growth journey, not that I am anyone special in that respect. I'm just an ordinary person whose life experiences have opened my eyes to Jesus at an early point in my young adult life due to certain circumstances. I am so grateful for what has happened in my life and that I was chosen worthy by Jesus to suffer through extreme emotional pain. This has directly led me towards Him. My mom's death was absolutely the worst thing that has ever happened to me; yet in retrospect, it was absolutely the best thing that has ever happened to me. This stark dichotomy remains quite perplexing to me. But I have always wanted to learn what the truth is.

My typical poetry style is to tell an impactful story with powerful emotional details that describe a specific defined topic; and most of them possess some rhythm and rhyming pattern based on the melodies of contemporary music. My hope is that they inspire and speak to you and specifically the younger generation— who might appreciate this form of expression. Most of my poems have been adapted as such, changing the lyrics of these songs to reveal important Bible truths. These melodies are also referenced next to my poem titles. But all of these poems are stand-alone, in that without the melody, they should still make perfect sense. Most of my poems are nonfictional (based on real-life experiences as either being autobiographical or biographical in context); while some are completely fictional (made-up to highlight a particular truth). None of these types really matter in order to highlight the main theme of each poem, nor have these been revealed. One secret I have learned over the years about growing closer to Christ is found in Rom 10:17: "So then faith *comes* by hearing, and hearing by the word of God" (NKJV, italics original). This can be accomplished in many ways and whichever ways you choose; these are pleasing to Him.

I considered my life pretty normal growing up until my mom's death. Then seemingly overnight, my world fell apart, and I felt lost and confused. I didn't know what was happening to me. I asked typical questions like, Why me? and, Why now?, but nothing was revealed to me. Shortly thereafter, my stepfather struggled with alcoholism as a way to self-medicate and numb the emotional pain that he was feeling. And the four of us kids were left to fend for ourselves for our own survival.

I returned to college but barely passed the remaining semesters of my first degree. Nothing as serious as this has ever occurred to me before or ever since thankfully. I was surviving one day at a time and learning valuable lessons as I went through the grieving process internally and privately. It was a slow process for me, as I was still learning who I was, developing into who I wanted to become, all while being a young teenager at heart. All of a sudden, I had to grow up and do so really fast . . . and on my own. Poetry was the only thing that worked for me. Back then, no one had cell phones, and the internet was just created a few years prior to this. Moreover, all of my childhood friends were back in my hometown or away at another college. None of my new college acquaintances could understand what I was going through. Indeed, I felt all alone. Poetry was my only outlet. Putting my emotions down on paper seemed to give these abstract things actual weight, relevance, and true acknowledgment. It also allowed me to literally (physically) and figuratively (emotionally) store my emotions away—as if to feel them, deal with them, learn from them, and then move on from them.

My original intention was simply to try to heal myself—deep down knowing that if I continued to bottle up these emotions over time, I would eventually explode just like a boiling pot of water in a kettle on the stovetop. Introverts need time, privacy, and quiet to process difficult experiences. I did not trust anyone enough to share these vulnerabilities with—for fear of judgment, criticism, or simply being dismissed. I never thought my poems would ultimately be worthy of sharing with others to help them in some way. In the midst of tragedy, you can only think of yourself. However, once you pass through that tragedy, you eventually regain a sense of others in the world and can see life and future possibilities and new opportunities more clearly. My hope and prayers are that my poems can help some of you in whatever you are facing today, whether it be serious or trivial, permanent or temporary, or spiritual, psychosocial, and/or physical. I now realize that Jesus was the only one who could heal me and not as a result of my own efforts. My efforts only proved to be futile attempts to try to do what only God can do. I have learned this valuable lesson to let go of certain things that I cannot control.

I have continued writing poetry on a regular basis about life's many experiences, topics, and questions. It has become and remains to be a strong coping mechanism for me when dealing with "life." I have continued to develop and refine my writing abilities and have strengthened my art by adding, practicing, and improving on many tools in my toolbox, so to speak. Sharing these Christian poems has become my priority given today's troubling times with so many broken and lost people. Jesus is the answer to all of your questions!

Introduction

Welcome to the fourth volume of my Christian poetry collection. It is entitled *Let Me Protect You: Poetic Bible Truths About Evil*. This collection focuses on evil and its consequences such as rebellion, pride, Satan, disease, death, and hell.

The first section in this book begins with rebellion. God is the boss. He is the Creator. He makes the rules. His rules for us are the Ten Commandments. These are His standards and/ or expectations for our behavior. These are His will. But we are human and imperfect. And God is Holy. In James 2:10, if you obey every law except one, then you are still guilty of breaking them all. It's an all or none kind of deal. We do not get any say or input. If we are guilty, then we deserve punishment, as the wages of sin is death (Rom 6:23). Rebellion is simply our stubbornness not to obey God. Jesus said, "If you love me, you will obey my commandments" (John 14:15 ESV).

The second section describes pride. Pride is placing ourselves and self-interests first above others and above God's will. We are our own boss. We know how to fix things. Pride is a very deadly sin because, again, it's a form of rebellion from God and assigning excellence and glory to ourselves instead of Him. Pride is exactly why Jesus was so critical of the Pharisees calling them a "brood of vipers" (Matt 12:34, 23:33 ESV). Jesus did not hate them, but rather He loved them tremendously because He wanted them to see that their pride was blocking their salvation. They were not the gatekeepers to God.

The third section depicts Satan. Evil exists in this world and the originator is Satan. All that is bad such as suffering, illness, and death come from him. Satan is not an equal to God; as God created him (Lucifer) as one of the archangels to protect His holiness. Yet he also rebelled from God thinking he could take His place in the heavens and sit on God's throne (Isa 14:12–15). Our battles in this world are not against flesh and blood but against the spiritual forces of evil in the heavenly realms (Eph 6:12). Yes, right now Satan has control of this world, and yes, he is in this world today. But soon, he will be cast away into the lake of fire when Jesus returns (Rev 20:10).

The fourth section deals with disease. Illness is the manifestation of sickness in our bodies. Our bodies are created from the dust of this world and will eventually return to the dust of this world. We are spiritual beings with a soul housed in flesh. When we die and once Jesus returns, believers will receive their new eternal bodies. But in the meantime, our bodies will break down because our bodies are of this world, and this world and everything associated with it has fallen. Many diseases are also a direct consequence of our own behavior, decisions, and choices, such as what we eat, how much we sleep, which toxins do we put into our bodies, and where we live and so forth. Yet other factors that contribute to disease we sometimes have little to no control over, such as autoimmune conditions, genetic predispositions, and chance exposures and accidents.

The fifth section highlights death. Everyone will die one day (Eccl 9:2–4). It's an absolute truth. No one can escape it—unless you are one of the select few who have been or will be raptured in the last days. Death is the consequence of our sin against God, our due punishment. Even nonbelievers will die. All humans will die. But we are eternal beings. The question is where will our souls/ spirits spend eternity? Believers will be in paradise in the presence of God Himself, whereas nonbelievers will reside in Hell forever apart from God and eventually be thrown into the lake of fire (Rev 20:15).

The final section focuses on hell. Hell is indeed the scariest place. You do not want to end up here. But unfortunately, many people will find themselves exactly here. The Bible predicts this (Matt 7:1–14).

Thank you and may God bless you. Please enjoy!

REBELLION

Staring into Temptation's Eyes

Once again, I find myself staring into temptation's
    eyes   1 Cor 10:13
Holding back, but looking at
All of the options which I must try
And the path I must choose before I die   Eph 5:15

When I stare into temptation's eyes
Desire soaks my blood
Urges appear, as well as some fear   Deut 10:12–22
So, then I ask "Why?" but soon answer, "Because."

When I stare into temptation's eyes
My future is foreseen
Needs disappear, and wants fill the air
Making me feed on lust, while addiction intervenes

When I stare into temptation's eyes
A craving drives my hunger
When I can hear my death when it's near
My heart begins to race for my days are numbered   Gen 6:3

Once again, I find myself staring into temptation's eyes
Sweating much, and shaking such
That I know temptation will entice
And take me with it on my final ride   Rom 6:23

Fear the LORD

(Adapted from the melody of "Calabria 2007" by Enur, feat. Natasja)

The fear of the LORD is the beginning of wisdom	Prov 9:10
The fear of the LORD is the beginning of wisdom	
Your kingdom come, Your will be done	Matt 6:10
The fear of the LORD is the beginning of wisdom	
The fear of the LORD is the beginning of wisdom	
Your kingdom come, Your will be done	

Respect and reverence should be vowed	Eph 5:20–21
God's the creator; we're not—hands down	Gen 1:1
Respect and reverence should be vowed	
God's the creator; we're not—hands down	

Respect and reverence should be vowed
God's the creator; we're not—hands down
Respect and reverence should be vowed
God's the creator; we're not—hands down

The fear of the LORD is the beginning of wisdom	
One day we will all be summoned to His throne	Rom 14:10–12
If in the Book of Life your name is not found	Ps 69:27–28
Without the blood of Jesus, you'll be hell bound	Rev 20:15
Account for yourself and then fire and brimstone	Rev 20:11–13
Plunged into the eternal unknown	
You'll be humbled, fall down and stumble	
You're in deep trouble; there's no more rebuttal	

God warns this fact	Rev 14:7
You're not big, but little	Prov 16:5
Ready for dismissal, you're indeed brittle	
His judgment will be the last	Heb 9:27
You need an acquittal	1 John 2:1
Yes, you're in a pickle headed for a committal	
Don't be condemned	Rom 5:12–21

The fear of the LORD is the beginning of wisdom
The fear of the LORD is the beginning of wisdom
Your kingdom come, Your will be done

Respect and reverence should be vowed
God's the creator; we're not—hands down
Respect and reverence should be vowed
God's the creator; we're not—hands down
Respect and reverence should be vowed
God's the creator; we're not—hands down
Respect and reverence should be vowed
God's the creator; we're not—hands down

You don't know it all, don't express gall
Pride will ultimately be your downfall   Prov 8:13
You won't be ready for the knuckleball
All in all, you start to quiver and bawl
You're defeated and resign
You've been judged by the divine
A dark tunnel appears and then a funnel
Then a loud rumble, there's no more struggle

God warns this fact
You're not big, but little
Ready for dismissal, you're indeed brittle
His judgment will be the last
You need an acquittal
Yes, you're in a pickle headed for a committal
Don't be condemned

The fear of the LORD is the beginning of wisdom
The fear of the LORD is the beginning of wisdom
Your kingdom come, Your will be done

The fear of the LORD is the beginning of wisdom
The fear of the LORD is the beginning of wisdom
Your kingdom come, Your will be done

Respect and reverence should be vowed
God's the creator; we're not—hands down
Respect and reverence should be vowed
God's the creator; we're not—hands down

You Will Reap What You Sow

(Adapted from the melody of "Good Ones" by Charli XCX)

You can have leisure for a season	
But sin will cause you to weaken	Rom 6:23
There will be consequences for sure	John 3:16–18
You will always reap what you sow	Gal 6:7–9

Don't blame others, just look in the mirror	Rom 14:11–13
Self-control is a fruit of the Spirit	Gal 5:22–23
God will not be mocked, this He spoke	Gal 6:7
You will always reap what you sow	

Be careful if you are constantly seeking pleasure	
You might be sentenced to hell forever	2 Thess 1:9
If you're a hypocrite and practice lawlessness,	
then woe	Matt 23:27–28
You will always reap what you sow	

You will always reap what you sow
You will reap what you sow
You will reap what you sow

If you're always compromising	
With no morals, it's not surprising	
At any time, God could send a deathblow	Sam 6; Acts 12:23
You will always reap what you sow	

Be careful if you are constantly seeking pleasure
You might be sentenced to hell forever
If you're a hypocrite and practice lawlessness, then woe
You will always reap what you sow

You will always reap what you sow
You will reap what you sow
You will reap what you sow

Be careful if you are constantly seeking pleasure
You will always reap what you sow
You might be sentenced to hell forever
You will reap what you sow

What Makes God Sad

(Adapted from the melody of "Landslide" by Fleetwood Mac)

God created you to wear a crown	2 Tim 2:12
But you chose rebellion and made Him frown	1 Sam 12:14–15
You lived your entire life so selfishly and just for yourself	1 Cor 10:24
Not much time left to turn it around	

Oh, now He's been sobbing from high above
When will you ever realize that enough is enough?
He loves you so much that He gave you countless
chances   John 3:16
But you never ask questions even though He has all the answers
       Jas 1:5

Well, it's not necessarily where you begin	
But rather exactly where you end	Matt 12:36–37
It's not that you're a smoker	
But that you've turned your shoulder	
To Him who has sacrificed everything for you	Rom 5:8

He respects your free will to determine	Gal 5:13
Where you prefer eternity to spend	
He wishes you were closer	Jas 4:7–10
Reachable if you were sober	
But the devil has certainly tricked you	John 8:44
But the devil has certainly tricked you	

He forgives no matter what	Heb 8:12
But you fell victim to another who's corrupt	2 John 1:7
Jesus said there's only one thing that can never be forgiven	
Denying the Holy Spirit, you'll be shunned	Matt 12:31–32

Oh, now He's been sobbing from high above
He's blessed you with grace, given you what you didn't deserve,
   beloved   John 1:16–17
He gave you life, shared special gifts, and directed your
   path   Prov 3:6
But you never gave Him a chance and you never gave anything
   back   John 15:5

Oh-oh, take His love, but you look down   Acts 4:12
Oh-oh, He cherishes your soul, but now it's bound
                                          Matt 25:31–46

If you'd refuse to surrender to your flesh, He'd fulfill   Rom 12:21
Well, for this time; evil has won
If you'd refuse to surrender to your flesh, then He would fulfill
Well, for this time; evil has won
Well, well, for this time; evil has won

For Those Who Abandon God, Eventually He Will Abandon Them

*(Adapted from the melody of "Better Days" by Mae Muller, Neiked &
Polo G)*

My family has disowned me
As if they didn't know me
Kept their distance remotely

They refuse to be persuaded
I always feel degraded
Thus, I stay barricaded

I've been isolated too long   Heb 10:25
I don't know exactly where I belong
It's so much easier to withdraw
What have I sown, I've sown, I've sown, I've sown?   Gal 6:7–8

It wasn't just a phase; I have breasts when I gaze
But I prefer to see a man in the mirror anyways
God must've made a mistake, He's such a comedian   Gen 1:27
But now I'm in control, I'm transgendered nowadays

I don't mean to offend
But you have a serious disease from your ovary that extends
How ironic I'm afraid, you must feel betrayed; but your future
    will all depend

Your malignancy has spread beyond your pelvis throughout
You're dying from a female cancer no doubt
You can deny all you want, but you must grapple
With the reality of what you're not, baffled?

Life has thrown you a curve ball
Your creator targeted with gall
I'm sorry you've been blackballed
This is possibly punishment for your stonewall   Rev 22:12

Surely, pride's the crime despite   Prov 8:13; Prov 16:5
Denying God's authority and foresight   Luke 12:9
Thinking you can define what's trite
When in fact it's His inherent right   Isa 40:23

It wasn't just a phase; I have breasts when I gaze
But I prefer to see a man in the mirror anyways
God must've made a mistake, He's such a comedian
But now I'm in control, I'm transgendered nowadays

I'm in control, in control, I think
I'm transgendered nowadays
I want to escape
I'm transgendered, transgendered

I'm transgendered nowadays
But I prefer to see a man in the mirror anyways
I'm transgendered nowadays
But I prefer to see a man in the mirror anyways

Worse Than Before

(Adapted from the melody of "Bad Dream" by Cannons)

We're all on a downward spiral
Have you seen what's gone viral?
All that's on our phone is so vile
Our culture today defiles

I have so many unanswered questions
And there's just no debate
Can I get you to agree?
When we disobey, we're prey   Eph 5:6

It's so much worse than before, it seems
It's so much worse than before, it's so extreme

Everybody lives so carefree
Right is wrong and wrong is right, you see   Isa 5:20
There's a consequence by His decree   Rom 6:23
And it'll be a deathblow   1 John 3:8

Erased; the Bible we must preserve
You can't just negate
You're going to have to trust me
When I say you'll be enslaved   Rom 6:6

It's so much worse than before, it seems
It's so much worse than before, it's so extreme
Everything on TV's so obscene

It's so much worse than before, it's so extreme
It's so much worse than before, it seems
It's so much worse than before, it's so extreme
Everything on TV's so obscene

It's so much worse than before, it's so extreme
It's so much worse than before, it seems

Blasphemous

(Adapted from the melody of "Glamorous" by Fergie, feat. Ludacris)

Feeling empty?
Do you confess that God sits on His throne?   Rom 10:9–11
Do you confess that God sits on His throne?
B-L-A-S-PH-EM-O-U-S yeah, B-L-A-S-PH-EM-O-U-S

Ask yourself this question: Do you deny that God's in charge?
Who do you rely? And what else do you maintain?   Rev 13:1
Is it blasphemous? Ooh, possibly, possibly

It's blasphemous, it's blasphemous, blasphemous
Is it blasphemous? Ooh, possibly, possibly
It's blasphemous, it's blasphemous, blasphemous
Is it blasphemous? Ooh, possibly, possibly

God's the king of all kings	Rev 17:14
He created angels and their wings	Ps 148; Col 1:1–29
He made the seasons and the spring	Gen 1:1–14
Love and holiness He brings	1 John 4:7–9; Rev 4:8

He's certain to intervene	Rom 8:26
Jesus Christ's our go-between	Col 1:15–16
He died as such to make us clean	1 Cor 15:3–8
So that you can achieve all your dreams	

The Spirit wants to indwell	1 Cor 6:19
Guide you, not compel	Ps 32:8
He gave you a free will	Gal 5:13
But the consequence might be hell	Rom 13:2

Don't focus on yourself—vanity	Gal 6:3
Focus on others and their calamities	John 13:34
Being present and listening	
Surrender and simply trust Him	Prov 3:5–6

Ask yourself this question: Do you deny that God's in charge?
Who do you rely? And what else do you maintain?

Is it blasphemous? Ooh, possibly, possibly
It's blasphemous, it's blasphemous, blasphemous
Is it blasphemous? Ooh, possibly, possibly
It's blasphemous, it's blasphemous, blasphemous
Is it blasphemous? Ooh, possibly, possibly

Be careful of your beliefs, especially those that are too extreme
You're not the boss, and you're not even supreme
You're made in the image of God, so it's best not to cuss Gen 1:26
You're guilty and in need of a savior with all that lust
                                                        Rom 1:18–32

You are destined to perish; as we're born with so much
    blemish   Rev 21:8
Only Jesus can replenish; this fact will never diminish   John 14:6
All the unbelievers will groan   Rev 20:15
Without Jesus, your fate's unknown
Do you confess that God sits on His throne?

B-L-A-S-PH-EM-O-U-S yeah, B-L-A-S-PH-EM-O-U-S

Ask yourself this question: Do you deny that God's in charge?
Who do you rely? And what else do you maintain?
Is it blasphemous? Ooh, possibly, possibly

It's blasphemous, it's blasphemous, blasphemous
Is it blasphemous? Ooh, possibly, possibly
It's blasphemous, it's blasphemous, blasphemous
Is it blasphemous? Ooh, possibly, possibly

Why live with all this fear? We only have so many years

Gen 6:3

You're not your own, there's nothing that you are
    owed   1 Cor 6:19–20
I'm sorry I have to be so frank, but what Kool-Aid did you drink?
Want your life to be in vain? Your legacy erodes

Do you want to fade away? Or do you desire
    doomsday?   Matt 12:36–37
You exist in the flesh and just go with the flow   Rom 8:8–9
You resist to be controlled, your choices are opposed
You will reap what you sow, don't be considered a foe   Gal 6:7

Do you confess that God sits on His throne?
You will reap what you sow
You will reap what you sow
Do you confess that God sits on His throne?
If not, then woe   Matt 12:31

Can't Break Free

(Adapted from the melody of "Sweater Weather" by The Neighborhood)

Since time began just as You planned   Gen 1:1
Created the world in a seven-day span   Gen 2:1–3
Yet the torment, this is man
Rebellion now limiting his lifespan   Gen 6:3

Selfishness seeking pleasure   Jas 3:16
Yet a present-day debtor
Their lives in their palms, distracted however
Everything's offensive, so perverse
Without Your laws and without remorse   1 John 1:10

Look at me now, check me out
Swipe right on my tinder account
Hold up, chill out
Come over, hand out?
Drugged up, passed out
The next day, down and out
No need to discuss or try to straighten out tonight
Satan's got a stranglehold   1 John 3:8; John 8:44
Can't break free
From him, but it's foretold
You have to read your Bible
The end is so much better   Rev 22

Every day, I've purposefully gone astray   Jas 4:17
It's pretty obvious, no need to convey
By design, despite my eyes, I'm blind   Rev 3:17
Unbeknownst to me, I'm sitting prey   1 Pet 5:8

My spirit's on fire, ablaze
My innocence has now vanished, erased
I carry a cross in case
I still cling to hope that I'm not a disgrace

Yeah, your direction ignored
I thought I knew You once before   Matt 7:23
But I can't hear you anymore
I need to be restored   1 Pet 5:10

Look at me now, check me out
Swipe right on my tinder account
Hold up, chill out
Come over, hand out?
Drugged up, passed out
The next day, down and out
No need to discuss or try to straighten out tonight
Satan's got a stranglehold
Can't break free
From him, but it's foretold
You have to read your Bible
The end is so much better

Promiscuity

(Adapted from the melody of "Bring It All To Me" by Blaque)

Just one man and one woman is God's decree   Matt 19:4–6
So that you can live your lives authentic and carefree

     Matt 11:28–30

Are you looking for proof?
Words of wisdom for you to declare
Straight from God Himself
He warns of the hazards to beware, truly

Beware: promiscuity
Death and destruction are some of the things that this
     will bring   1 Cor 6:18
Learn to go with His flow   John 16:13
Beware: promiscuity
Jealousy and hardships will occur coincidentally   Gal 5:19–21

Beware: what's your zeal?
What do these compromises to your fleshly desires
     reveal?   Rom 8:13–14
Soon, you'll find out how these things make you feel
Years, this could steal   Rom 6:23
Fevers and nightmares, waking up to screams
Is this surreal?
Eventually, the truth will no longer be concealed   John 8:31–32

Beware: promiscuity
Guilt and addiction are some of the things that this
     will bring   Thess 5:6–8
Learn to go with His flow
Beware: promiscuity
Depression and torment will occur coincidentally

     Rev 20:10

This place where you reside will collide with God's best plan for
    you   Jer 29:11
When will it all subside?
There are consequences and He can cease to provide
Especially if you continue to live this way despite, truly   Heb 9:27

Beware: promiscuity
Shame and infections are some of the things that this
    will bring   Mark 8:38
Learn to go with His flow
Beware: promiscuity
Loneliness and sorrow will occur coincidentally   2 Cor 7:10

Beware: promiscuity
Angst and upheaval are some of the things that this
    will bring   Isa 35:4
Learn to go with His flow
Beware: promiscuity
Frustration and unrest will occur coincidentally   Matt 11:28

Science???

(Adapted from the melody of "November Rain" by Guns N' Roses)

Even though you love another man, I can see you're without
    shame   Lev 18:22
It's impossible to procreate in nature, can you explain?
Your science is actually anti-science, so perverted
    and profane   1 Cor 6:9–11
It's pride and it's rebellion; this is not what God's ordained
                                                      Prov 16:5

You promote abortion before one's birth, "pro-choice" you
    exclaim
For God said, "I knew you before I formed you in your mother's
    womb to be a prophet one day"
I chose your birthday   Jer 1:5
Now you want children the power to define which gender they
    prefer over their chromosomes that God assigned by design
As if to spit in His face, an act full of disdain
That you would know any better; this is not what God's ordained
                                                  Gen 1:27

You must be evil; you must atone   Eph 1:7
This is just the devil seeking God's throne   Isa 14:12–15
You should pray that God chooses to postpone   2 Pet 3:9
But rather I pray that Jesus returns quickly home   Acts 1:11

People have become lovers of themselves   2 Tim 3:2
This is the prophecy of the last days
Today, much of what we see foretells disobedience
As too many will not be saved   Matt 7:13

You must be evil; you must atone
This is just the devil seeking God's throne
You should pray that God chooses to postpone
But rather I pray that Jesus returns quickly home

You try to control the language and our thoughts, so insane
You do everything in your power to strip our freedoms, constrain
You use Alinsky tactics, predictable and germane
You can never replace God; this is not what God's ordained

Heb 13:8

So, you think your progressive beliefs are compliant with science?
But science can only describe what is natural
The Almighty, though, is supernatural   Rom 8:6–11
He is outside of time and above and beyond the natural

Gen 1:14–19

His existence you can't even entertain
And thus, you are truly ignorant

Blatant Disobeying

(Adapted from the melody of "Constant Craving" by k.d. lang)

What I witness as I gaze	
Outward disease from within	Exod 15:26
With what used to be delayed	
Today, judgment begins	Rom 2:1–3

By blatant disobeying
His protection's rescinded

Feeling great loss of control	
Trying to find any excuse	
Relying solely on yourself	Matt 19:26–28
God expresses His disapproval	Prov 6:16–19

Blatant disobeying	
Death is the price of sin	Rom 6:23

Disobeying His laws—blatant disobeying
Death is the price of sin
Death is the price of sin

They are clueless; I'm amazed	
His patience starts to thin	
Over and over, God feels so betrayed	Matt 26:23–24
Evil, He allows in	Isa 48:10–11

By blatant disobeying
His protection's rescinded

God desires deeply for you to know	
That He's the source of all truth	John 14:6
But it's your decision if you rebel	Gal 5:13
Yet, He determines the final rebuke	Rom 14:10

Blatant disobeying
Death is the price of sin

Disobeying His laws—blatant disobeying
Death is the price of sin
Death is the price of sin

Some people are no longer afraid
Their defiance is shown when
In the flesh, they're never ashamed   Luke 13:3
Ignorant and predestined   1 Cor 15:34

By blatant disobeying
His protection's rescinded

As such, you need a Savior; it's so   Rom 3:23
His tolerance, don't confuse   2 Pet 3:9
God wants the best for you, now you know   Ps 103:8
For there will be no excuse   Rom 1:20

Blatant disobeying
Death is the price of sin

Disobeying His laws—blatant disobeying
Death is the price of sin
Death is the price of sin

Blatant disobeying
Death is the price of sin

Disobeying His laws—blatant disobeying
God wants to be your companion   Ps 89:15
God wants to be your friend   John 15:15
On His goodness depend   Matt 6:31–33
You are loved, not condemned   1 John 4:9–10

PRIDE

The Tower of Babel

(Adapted from the melody of "You Right" by Doja Cat & The Weeknd)

Across the earth, they had one speech	Gen 11:1
They found Shinar out from the east	Gen 10:10
To build a city and a tower	
Up to heaven whose top would reach	Gen 11:4
To show their greatness on display	Gen 11:4
Their prideful selves just to convey	
But God saw what they imagined to do	Gen 11:5
And confused their language in lieu	Gen 11:7
But yet, they traveled	
And built that, the Tower	
Of Babel, but then could not understand	
Each other, so they scattered	Gen 11:8
Across the face of the earth	Gen 11:9
Self-sufficiency and great power plays	
Up through the clouds to amaze	Gen 11:4
To build their own stairway	
Unsuccessful to their dismay	
Men and their flattery	
Find some more strategies	
But God stepped in to decrease	
To help man find peace	John 14:27
His ways we must keep	Isa 55:8–9
His results speak to critique	

Please listen to my decree
Holy I am, you must flee   Exod 3:5
Soon, there will be an appointee
But that's all I can say for now

Across the earth, they had one speech
They found Shinar out from the east
To build a city and a tower
Up to heaven whose top would reach

To show their greatness on display
Their prideful selves just to convey
But God saw what they imagined to do
And confused their language in lieu

But yet, they traveled
And built that, the Tower
Of Babel, but then could not understand
Each other, so they scattered
Across the face of the earth

Man has a false sense of ego, don't you agree?
This is reality
You must approach me humbly   1 Pet 5:6–7
But spiritually, you're actually devoid of life   Eph 2:1–10
Empty just like the Dead Sea
Think you're a VIP?

You have to receive my Sent One to come close to me   Rom 5:1–2
Become a new creation in Christ; that is the key   2 Cor 5:17
Without Him, you will be nothing—I foresee   John 15:4–5
Otherwise on bended knee, your requests are simply silent pleas
                                                                Phil 2:10–11

Across the earth, they had one speech
They found Shinar out from the east
To build a city and a tower
Up to heaven whose top would reach

To show their greatness on display
Their prideful selves just to convey
But God saw what they imagined to do
And confused their language in lieu

But yet, they traveled
And built that, the Tower
Of Babel, but then could not understand
Each other, so they scattered
Across the face of the earth

Blinded

So many people are hurting these days. Why can't they
  see You?   2 Cor 4:4
They listen closely to others' advice while they steal
  Your credit   Ps 118:8
Their suffering is so intense, the burdens they carry
  each day   Gal 6:2–12
They rely on their own thinking. Why can't they accept Your
  plan?   Jer 29:11
All things work out to be good in the end, even when the bad
  leads to good   Rom 8:28

You are the answer; You are the only doorway through   John 10:7
Please heal their blind eyes, open their hearts wide   Luke 24:45
To accept the limits of being human, unblind their blind eyes
They need You so much, but they've been taught not
  to see You   1 John 2:15–17
The truth is so powerful, dangerous to the oppressor   John 8:44

She cried herself to sleep each night, her thoughts fixed on small
  details
You are the light shining in the dark, she'll see You if she just
  opens her eyes   John 8:12
Why, why doesn't she seek You out? You're always there next to
  her   Heb 13:5
Your arms caress her, yet she's so clueless

I feel You; I see You; thank You for my sight   Matt 5:8
You are the source, I'm so grateful for Your gifts   1 Cor 8:6
I want You to work through me, my words provide
  comfort   Eph 2:10
I direct them to You to regain their coveted lost sight
I testify to the Truth, my experiences point to You   John 15:27

The bad, and now the good, just as You said

Those who walk close dwell in shelter   Ps 91:3–4
You are the Protector, as evil's always conspiring   Prov 11:19
Often times there is no rhyme or reason. It is what it is

Our attitudes tell the story: who's saved and who's lost   Matt 7:20
Too many leave without knowing You, lost souls in
   forgotten time   Matt 7:13
I pray I never lose my sight; I pray others' gain theirs   Ps 53:2
You are so wonderful, the good shepherd   John 10:11–14
You know what is best for us, let us trust in You   Ps 37:3–5

They think You are responsible for all, all the bad sticks to You
But You are really only good: no bad; never did,
   never will   Ps 103:8
It's never too late to gain sight, even if it's in the last minute
What a waste of life looking back, so many lost opportunities

It's not about me, it's all about others   John 15:12–13
It's love, caring, and helping; steering Your sheep   John 21:15–17

Skeptical

(Adapted from the melody of "Chemical" by Post Malone)

Many of us would prefer to go astray   Isa 53:6–12
When faced with the truth, some of us would rather
   downplay   1 John 1:8
Whether we agree or not, our death will come
   someday   Heb 9:27
But it all comes down to pride   Prov 11:2

Some have faith, but you refuse
You prefer to see the proof   John 20:25
Logical and reasoning until . . .

You're facing His glory, what'll be your excuse?   Rom 1:20
You're gonna feel His fury, what do you think He'll
   conclude?   John 3:36
Knees buckling, you're weary; damned to hell I presume Rev 21:8

How do you know for sure? You're skeptical
Suffer from grandeur? You're skeptical

You need a personal relationship, but this is strange   Rev 3:20
In order to receive His free divine exchange   Rom 3:23–24
It's not something that can be gauged; it simply can't be
   ascertained
Don't stand there and complain or your fate will be flames   Rev
     20:15

Some have faith, but you refuse
You prefer to see the proof
Logical and reasoning until . . .

You're facing His glory, what'll be your excuse?
You're gonna feel His fury, what do you think He'll conclude?
Knees buckling, you're weary; damned to hell I presume

34

How do you know for sure? You're skeptical
Mathematical? You're skeptical
Empirical? You're skeptical

Analytical? You're skeptical

You've been tricked to believe and accept what's false   Rev 12:9
Intellectual? You're skeptical

SATAN

Roaring Lion

(Adapted from the melody of "Heathens" by Twenty One Pilots)

Hidden from our vision, status quo	
Plotting our destruction from below	Ps 21:11
There's nothing left here to disprove	
A ravenous appetite to consume	1 Pet 5:8

Stalking all the time, apropos
Striking relentlessly, a mighty foe
Please don't brush it off with an excuse
He'll get inside your head and accuse   Rev 12:10

The adversary prowls around like a lion roaring to disobey on
    display   1 Pet 5:8
He uses anything he can to declare war
There's nothing he doesn't hate, so much rage

Most people are clueless, they don't have a clue
If you're not paying attention, His demons will
    subdue   Matt 12:43–45
Once they gain control, it's difficult to undo
You must be sober-minded and be watchful   1 Pet 5:8

Hidden from our vision, status quo
Plotting our destruction from below
There's nothing left here to disprove
A ravenous appetite to consume

Once you're in their clutches, say farewell
You need the LORD your God to expel   2 Pet 2:4
You needn't be a target, apprehension
We need to promote comprehension

Most people are clueless, they don't have a clue
If you're not paying attention, His demons will subdue
Once they gain control, it's difficult to undo
You must be sober-minded and be watchful

Hidden from our vision, status quo
Plotting our destruction from below
There's nothing left here to disprove
A ravenous appetite to consume

Stand with God, there's no need to be afraid   Isa 41:10
Use His Word, you don't have to fall to prey   Ps 23:4
Put on the armor of God and trust   Eph 6:11–12
Under His feet, Satan will be crushed   Gen 3:15; Rom 16:20

I Faced the Devil

(Adapted from the melody of "Graveyard" by Halsey)

So, let it begin:
You spoke right to my heart to be benevolent   Jer 33:3
Then it suddenly changed when
Down the stairs, she charged in
And questioned me, the money—I sinned
Angrily she remarked

Oh, I've learned to listen to your quiet voice
   teacher   John 10:27–28
I can't stop, and I follow your call   Heb 4:12
I keep trying, I keep trying, I keep trying

She says I can't do these things in your namesake
I faced the devil directly with a devout heart   Eph 6:13–17
Although I let go all the guilt you placed on me
For helping another when they needed—like a lifeguard

Oh, I've learned to listen to your quiet voice teacher
I can't stop hearing no matter how small
I keep resisting her efforts to subvert   Jas 4:7
Over the top until the exact hour

Just like when Jesus looked deep into Peter's eyes
And rebuked the devil, it's not his fault—it's a safeguard

                                              Matt 16:23

She was mad at me
Comparing this to her friend's death, she disagreed
She doesn't understand the circumstance

The devil's trying to steal
But You shut that door, Your Spirit speaks if you
   listen   Prov 3:6–16
The truth is soon revealed   John 14:6

Oh, I've learned to listen to your quiet voice teacher
I can't stop, and I follow your call
I keep trying, I keep trying, I keep trying

She said instead that I should forsake
I faced the devil directly with a devout heart
I know in my soul the devil's subtle ways have been decoded
There's no point in tracking the scorecard

Oh, 'cause I keep reminding myself I'm a believer   John 14:11–12
I'm not sure that You are her north star
I keep offering my faith to assert
Raised Catholic, but now she's bizarre

Oh, when you sow the seeds, your harvest will grow   Gal 6:7–8
It's so much easier to follow You and be favored

Oh, it's tragic how
Selfishness finds its way in and then divides   Jas 3:16

Oh, 'cause I keep rebuking the deceiver   Jas 4:7
Over the top until the exact hour
I keep running my race and assert   2 Tim 4:7
Over the top until the exact hour

Oh, when you're surrounded by the enemy   Luke 19:43
I take the condemnation and simply discard   Rom 8:1

Questions for God

(Adapted from the melody of "Experience (Live at FIP 2015)" by Ludovico Einaudi)

Why do we have this? Why does this exist?
Why does evil occur and why does it persist?
Why do You permit? How does this fit?   Rom 13:1–14
What's the premise and can we accept it?

How can we live in this world when tragedies are happening
  every day to some of us?
How can we live our lives focused on helping our fellow mankind
  when things are so unjust?
Too many times we've been burned by people and other
  circumstances that test our faith and too often disturb us.
How can we practice "good" while in this world with all the
  pressures and selfish drives that are designed just to divide?

Please help me understand and accept Your master plan that
  You've been supplying compassion ever since time began.
How can we learn to withstand all the evil that exists in this land
  and find some kind of meaning and purpose today, right now
  other than
what we experience every day, the crimes and justice that never
  came, the suffering around, numb to death, and the loss of our
  humanity?
How can we seek immortality while our culture continues to
  decline rapidly because of vengeful attacks by Satan to discredit
  and defile Christianity?

We indeed need You, please save all of us; time is running out, it's
  time that we start to shout.
I believe in You, please protect us; I'm waiting for the trumpet
  sound to be lifted into the clouds.

Why is it that You <u>allow</u> and honor their free <u>will</u> given so many
people have chosen for themselves to go their own way and
blatantly <u>rebel</u>?
Why don't you call Your <u>angels</u> who will appear and quickly <u>expel</u>
those who won't be <u>compelled</u> to change their course and bid
<u>farewell</u>?

Why do "good" people have to live alongside those who hate
others and who hurt others and who obviously don't seem to
<u>care</u>?
Is it that there are no "good" people and that we are all unworthy
of Your righteousness and all of us fall short in such <u>despair</u>?

How can I be <u>used</u> instead of "those who <u>accuse</u>" to help fulfill
Your purpose and convince people to boldly approach <u>You</u>?
And if they <u>refuse</u>, eventually judgment will <u>ensue</u>, and they'll
be thrown into the Lake of Fire where they will ultimately be
<u>consumed</u>.
Is the answer to use love and understanding to combat
evil wherever and whenever it <u>exists</u> and in every single
<u>circumstance</u>?
Is it wise to surrender our life so that we can be used in <u>contrast</u>
to role model and to represent You well to others then <u>perhaps</u>?

But for those who remain <u>proud</u> and for those who prefer to
<u>turnabout</u>, they will be cursed no <u>doubt</u>, but I know that You
will certainly <u>allow</u>
them to live their lives <u>throughout</u> this earthly existence <u>without</u>
the possibility of heaven and an eternity with You <u>endowed</u>.

Why is there cancer and <u>AIDS</u>, tornados and <u>earthquakes</u>, all
forms of addiction and abuse, pornography, murder, and <u>rape</u>,
mass shootings and police <u>mistakes</u>, and abortions just <u>in case</u>,
droughts, famines, and gang violence, theft, and <u>heartache</u>?
Why are there car <u>accidents</u>, genocide, poverty, <u>homelessness</u>,
starvation, wars, suicide, devil worship, and <u>loneliness</u>?

Why is there <u>forgetfulness</u>, volcanos and <u>paralysis</u>, drownings,
    animal cruelty, mutilations, and <u>negligence</u>?

Why do we have <u>this</u>? Why does this <u>exist</u>?
Why does evil occur and why does it <u>persist</u>?
Why do You <u>permit</u>? How does this <u>fit</u>?
What's the <u>premise</u> and can we <u>accept it</u>?

Oh my gosh!
Why is there tech <u>addiction</u>, floods, tsunamis, carbon <u>emissions</u>,
    birth defects, terminal diseases, and exorbitant college <u>tuition</u>?
Why are there <u>politicians</u>, heart disease, mental <u>illness</u>, incest,
    divorce <u>petitions</u>, PTSD, and gender <u>definitions</u>?
Why is there <u>autism</u>, and all sorts of <u>racism</u>, fraud and <u>terrorism</u>,
    dictatorships, and <u>communism</u>?
Why is there <u>pollution</u>, child <u>prostitution</u>, the theory of <u>evolution</u>,
    and forced wealth <u>redistribution</u>?

An Angel of Light in Disguise

(Adapted from the melody of "In Your Eyes" by Robin Schulz, feat. Alida)

You think that everything's alright
Just because outside it's bright
But beware, it's not true

The devil seeks to trick your brain   1 John 4:1
Doesn't want you to ascertain
So, you won't learn the truth   John 8:44

He will constantly deny
You'll know him by his replies
The Word of God, he's opposed   Isa 8:20

A master of deception to confuse
If you're not careful, he'll subdue   1 John 3:8
He's lurking in the shadows

He's there looking for any chance to spar
To make you take his mark   Rev 13:11–18

Your destruction he relentlessly contrives   2 Thess 2:9–10
He wants you misinformed
Consider yourself warned

An angel of light in disguise   2 Cor 11:13–15
In disguise
An angel of light in disguise
In disguise
An angel of light in disguise
An angel of light in disguise

He wants <u>his</u> name proclaimed   Isa 14:12–24
The LORD God's name in vain   Exod 20:7
He wants you to be deprived

He wants your eyes to become blind
He wants to steal your birthright   Gen 25:29–34
He wants to bring you down

He will constantly deny
You'll know him by his replies
The Word of God, he's opposed

A master of deception to confuse
If you're not careful, he'll subdue
He's lurking in the shadows

He's there looking for any chance to spar
To make you take his mark

Your destruction he relentlessly contrives
He wants you misinformed
Consider yourself warned

An angel of light in disguise
In disguise
An angel of light in disguise
In disguise
An angel of light in disguise
An angel of light in disguise

An angel of light in disguise
In disguise
An angel of light in disguise
In disguise
An angel of light in disguise

Love of the Truth vs. The Deception of the Devil

(Adapted from the melody of "Long Flight" by Future Islands)

The devil perverts everything God does	Acts 13:10
All he can do is imitate	
In the beginning, God created the stars	Gen 1:1

God etched His Son's story hidden in the constellations	Ps 19
Then He created angels and light by His word	Gen 1:3

Lucifer was once a beautiful being	Ezek 28:11–19
But now he influences sex and drugs and rock and roll	Ezek 28:13

God used His mouth to create all things
Whereas the devil subtly programs our language for defeat

God created sex purposefully	Gen 1:28
Designed it to be complimentary between one man and one woman for pleasure	

Today, countless sexual perversions exist; enough of that said	1 John 3:8
God created each of us a man or a woman	Gen 1:27

But today, many people question God	Isa 55:8–9
As if He made some mistake	
People think they have a right to choose their gender identities	
People are so wrong	

God created true health and wellness until sin entered this world	Rom 5:12
Now there's aging, suffering, disease, and death	Rom 6:23

The fruits of the spirit are bountiful   Gal 5:22–23
But the devil steers people in the opposite direction   Rom 14:23
Hate, anger, stress, impatience, and selfishness—unfaithfulness
    and addiction

God commands His angels; the devil directs his
    demons   Ps 91:11–12
The devil created astrology to influence some kind of meaning for
    people who are seeking answers

God holds three awesome numbers: 3, 5, and 7   John 14:26; John
                                    1:16; Gen 1, 2:1–2
The devil boasts his three: 666—known as the mark of the beast
                                           Rev 13

God gives us free will, whereas the devil uses this to create
    bondage in our lives
With the antichrist, Satan and the false prophet—The Holy
    Trinity's plagiarized

The devil perverts everything that God does
All he can do is desecrate
God is omniscient, omnipresent, and omnipotent
The devil can only anticipate

And God is light   1 John 1:5
While the devil will transform into an angel of
    light just to deceive   2 Cor 11:13–15
Jesus was resurrected after the third day according to
    God's plan   Luke 24:6–7
And in the last days, the fatal wound of one of the heads of the
    beast will be healed   Rev 13:3

DISEASE

Enduring Grief

(Adapted from the melody of "play w/ me" by Bailey Bryan)

Since I was young, I've hidden this scar
It quickly appeared out of nowhere, was thrust upon   Isa 30:20–21
For a healthy boy, it was quite bizarre
Now, I have an idea that describes this phenomenon

Back then, no clue; I had to face the truth
I couldn't find the words   Phil 4:5–7
Not sure what ensued, but my thyroid grew
Sadly, I was never heard

So, emotional trauma linking to my physical injury
It's legitimate; this has been my reality
Coming to terms with my Mother who was suddenly deceased
One scary predicament   Ps 34:18

Torment brewing and concealed internally
Trembling hands turning into a fast heartbeat
Losing weight and not tolerating the heat
Something's wrong with me; you face disease when you endure
    grief

Torment brewing and concealed internally
Trembling hands turning into a fast heartbeat
Losing weight and not tolerating the heat
Something's wrong with me; you face disease when you endure
    grief

Wondering where all this came from   2 Cor 4:16–18
I spent hours feeling numb
Suspecting a trap and possibly destruction perhaps
Thus, I concluded: I must control my attitude
My mind and spirit were renewed   Eph 4:23

Emotional trauma linking to my physical injury
It's legitimate; this has been my reality
Coming to terms with my Mother who was suddenly deceased
I questioned being a Christian   Jas 1:2–4

Torment brewing and concealed internally
Trembling hands turning into a fast heartbeat
Losing weight and not tolerating the heat
Something's wrong with me; you face disease when you endure
    grief

Torment brewing and concealed internally
Trembling hands turning into a fast heartbeat
Losing weight and not tolerating the heat
Something's wrong with me; you face disease when you endure
    grief

It's true; you face disease when you endure grief   1 Pet 5:10
It's true; you face disease when you endure grief

Fight

(Adapted from the melody of "Lights" by Ellie Goulding)

When you're a Christian, spiritual attacks will be thrown	John 16:33
Straight from Satan configured to make you groan	
Relentless he always is in an effort designed to deplete	
One thing after another purposefully just to defeat	

You have to fight these attacks firmly to dethrone	John 16:33
Realize that you're not alone	Isa 41:10
Words have power, reap what they have sown	Heb 4:12
You're victorious, let it be known	John 16:33

'Cause he's longing, longing, longing to roam	1 Pet 5:8
Causing, causing, causing doom	
You have to fight these attacks firmly to dethrone	
Realize that you're not alone	

Rely largely on the Word of God	Heb 4:12
But when things seem dim, put all your weight in prayer	Phil 4:6
And don't regret what's been for persecution is a privilege	Matt 5:10
Your faith can surely heal since Jesus provided the escape	1 Cor 10:13

You have to fight these attacks firmly to dethrone
Realize that you're not alone
Words have power, reap what they have sown
You're victorious, let it be known

'Cause he's longing, longing, longing to roam
Causing, causing, causing doom
You have to fight these attacks firmly to dethrone
Realize that you're not alone

Fight, fight, fight, fight, fight, fight, fight, fight
Fight, fight, fight, fight, fight, fight

You have to fight these attacks firmly to dethrone
Realize that you're not alone
Words have power, reap what they have sown
You're victorious, let it be known

'Cause he's longing, longing, longing to roam
Causing, causing, causing doom
You have to fight these attacks firmly to dethrone
Realize that you're not alone
Shalom, shalom

Fight, fight, fight, fight, fight, fight, fight, fight
Shalom, shalom

You Are What You Breathe

(Adapted from the melody of "MEIN TEIL (You Are What You Eat)" by Rammstein [edit remix by Pet Shop Boys])

People dropping left and right
Most are hiding day and night
Grocery stores turn into fights
Death ensues, no end in sight
Is this the end? Cannot defend

This is covid; you are what you breathe.
This is covid, covid-19

The virus travels through the air
Panic, chaos, worst nightmare
The world is dying people fear
All toilet paper disappears
You are what you breathe

Schools closing, children roam
Elderly folks staying home
On their couches laying prone
As if acquired the syndrome

Wall Street nervous, market crash
Rules emerging very fast
Social distance, no contact
No face to face, just internet
Is this the end? Cannot defend

This is covid; you are what you breathe.
This is covid, covid-19

Rising boredom, time persists
Shelter orders, make checklists
Frustration looms, fear resist
Does God love us? Does God exist?

This is covid; you are what you breathe.
This is covid, covid-19

Help

(Adapted from the melody of "Time" by NF)

Even if we don't wanna work tonight
And most say we're crazy
But we go to work anyway
We know we'll get through all this despite
We'll be here braving
This covid we're facing
We just need

An opportunity to show that we're worthy
We know that this will be a difficult journey
We're all stressed out, for any possible cure we're searching
Nationally, we're probably worse than we thought, that's what
    we're learning

Coronavirus is the cause why these folks are dying
Every day we witness something more horrifying
Acting like we've not, but we push it down hiding
We don't like to feel helpless, which we know we're denying

And when we think all is good, all of a sudden another patient
    codes
That we're doing all we can and when we're done, we do some
    more
That's just our drive taking over, 'cause this profession has
    bestowed
We're the definition of tough when there's a loss of control

It comes out of each of us when you realize that you cannot
    reverse fate
We want to take away the pain and let our empathy showcase
When you're dismayed, we'll be there beside you and likely
    embrace
But whatever awaits, we're gonna fight this until it fades

Even if

Even if we don't wanna work tonight
And most say we're crazy
But we go to work anyway
We know we'll get through all this despite
We'll be here braving
This covid we're facing
We just need

Help
We, we need help
We just need help
We, we just need help
Help, help

Yeah, just before this disease was named
We were fighting with each other with our political
    games   Mark 13:8
Everything shut down, life as we know it has changed
We never saw it coming with so many fingers to blame

Only time will tell, praying for the end of this thing
Thinking about life, and contemplating everything
Some are distressed, others scared, and still others are healing
Searching for answers that we know are hidden obviously

So many questions, what to think, most unknown previously
We've soaked through tissues from trying to fix them
Doing all we can but some of us are overwhelmed
When will an answer come? Messenger RNA vaccine proponents
And we carry these weights and then we share our condolences

Watching the news and all the death in the press
Lots of suffering, including our colleagues nevertheless
That's not what we envisioned; you know we want this to end

Even if

Even if we don't wanna work tonight
And most say we're crazy
But we go to work anyway
We know we'll get through all this despite
We'll be here braving
This covid we're facing
We just need

Help
We, we need help
We just need help
We, we just need help
Help, help

DEATH

Not Wanting to Let Go

The passing of a friend, of a son, of a father,
Of a mother, or of a woman, of a man, or of a daughter
No matter which it is, or of whom of which we know
This occurrence of transition; we're not wanting to let go

The hardships that we face, the new path to which we climb
We struggle for any acceptance of death's fear to which we find
For the hours which we've spent all while the loved one has
    declined
We're introduced to exhaustion, and this we must keep in mind

Sadness is what we feel, the pool of tears that we shed
As might be anger or injustice, these are the scars which we must
    mend
Our love will serve to heal, all the love for which we send
To the lost one and to each other, this integration we depend

But death is like a wing, a gift of flight to the bird
To ascend to heights far beyond us, the dis-ease has just been
    cured
Tomorrow, though still dim, a new day will rise for sure
We grow, but seek one's remembrance, though the pain remains
    to endure

The passing of a friend, of a son, of a father,
Of a mother, or of a woman, of a man, or of a daughter
No matter which it is, or of whom of which we know
This occurrence of transition; we're not wanting to let go

Our Future Companion

DRUGS, SEX, ALCOHOL

TORNADOES, FLOODS, POLIO

HIT AND RUN AND BLOWN TIRES

EARTHQUAKES, BOMBINGS AND FOREST FIRES

MARIJUANA AND COCAINE

BUNGEE JUMPING AND GOING INSANE

CANCER, SMALLPOX, AND AIDS

MURDER, ROBBERY, AND RAIDS

MUGGING, HEART FAILURE, AND THEFT

DEATH TO ALL UNTIL THERE'S NO ONE LEFT

OVERDOSE AND FORCEFUL RAPE

HIJACKINGS; THERE'S NO ESCAPE

GANGBANGING AND LSD

SLEEPING PILLS AND CAFFEINE

SMOKING CRASHES (CAR AND TRAIN)

YOU, LIVING YOUR LIFE IN THE FAST LANE

DOA AND SUICIDE

DRIVE BY SHOOTINGS, ALONG FOR THE RIDE

DEATH IN ACCIDENTS

DEATH IN LEGAL SETTLEMENTS

DROWNING BY SUFFOCATION

NATURAL DEATH AND PARALYZATION

BOMBS AND GUNS AND EVEN KNIVES

THESE ARE THE ENDS OF ALL YOUR LIVES

tree shedding

The tree begins to shed
Some leaves are young, and some are old
The tree will always shed
In the summer when it's warm and during the fall months when
    it's cold

Some leaves are subject to disease
It is the pain that they will inflict
They poison all the healthy leaves
And induce each branch to become a stick

Some diseases will pollute the stem
They act so merciless in their disguise
They focus their attack directly onto them
Yet diseases are some of life's demise

Some leaves are prone to predators
They devour some of them whole
Predators will feed on each and every tip
Just to sample the leaf's body and soul

Some predators tear off the life source
Causing the leaves to be without a breath
They gnaw on the leaves with such relentless force
Yet predators are some of life's death

Some leaves are governed by the wind
It is nature who gets the blame
The wind will pull on every leaf
For it is the weak ones which it will claim

Some cold winds will yank on the leaf's grip
Persuading them that surrender is best
Yet they will all descend and journey their final trip
For nature is one of life's eternal rest

The tree begins to shed
Some leaves are young, and some are old
The tree will always shed
In the summer when it's warm and during the fall months when
it's cold

By My Side

Such a sad, sad situation
As my family and friends gather
Today on this solemn occasion
My youngest lay by my side

I only wish to observe from above
My body below so pale and cold
In this warm room filled with grief and love
There, my youngest lay by my side

It's too much for me to believe it's true
Thankful for living each day so full
I'm forever sorry I can't stay here with you
Though my youngest lay by my side

Displayed are pictures and pictures galore
My life as witnessed in print
All while, there stretched along the bench
My youngest lay by my side

I'm comforted by all those who cared
The flowers, the cards, and tears
The best coming from the stories shared
While my youngest lay by my side

Before touching up my hair and make-up
My girls plead one more time
Mommy, Mommy, please wake up
Still, my youngest lay by my side

I Miss You

(Adapted from the melody of "Don't Let Me Down" by Chainsmokers, feat. Daya)

I can't believe this is happening to you, to me, to us right now
Doesn't seem right, this can't be real
Why you? Why not someone else? You are so young and beautiful
Your entire life was in front of you

I walk in. You're lying still. The hospital room seems so cold and
    dark
I'm greeted by your mom and then your dad
Our friends stand there quietly, no one really knows exactly what
    to say
We're in such a deep, deep shock

I miss you; I miss you; I miss you right now
Yeah, I miss you right now
So don't let me, don't let me, don't let me frown
I think I'm losing my friend now
I'm in my bed trying to cope
We'll meet again soon I suppose
So don't let me, don't let me, don't let me frown
Don't let me frown, don't let me frown

We're sixteen, can't process these intense emotions with every
    second
I hope to wake up and see you smile
The tubes drain, the beeping sounds, a machine that takes one
    more breath for you
For how much longer with this last?

Six months ago, you were fine. Every day was like the day before
It seems like a distant memory
How rapidly things have changed, your body just a shell of your
    former self
We hold our breath as your pupils relax

I miss you; I miss you; I miss you right now
Yeah, I miss you right now
So don't let me, don't let me, don't let me frown
I think I'm losing my friend now
I'm in bed trying to cope
We'll meet again soon I suppose
So don't let me, don't let me, don't let me frown
Don't let me frown

I feel lost, can't concentrate; the tears keep streaming down my
    face
It hurts so much, just want it to stop
Everything reminds me of our friendship that was so strong
A concrete bond that will never break

I can't sleep. I hear your laugh. I look around but nowhere are you
    found
I wonder if you can still sense me
Today, we will bury you. None of us will ever be the same
Our love will always be remembered

I miss you; I miss you; I miss you right now
Yeah, I miss you right now
So don't let me, don't let me, don't let me frown
I think I'm losing my friend now
I'm in bed trying to cope
We'll meet again soon I suppose
So don't let me, don't let me, don't let me frown
Don't let me frown

It's so sad, I'll never see you grow up the way it's meant to be
All your milestones and victories
A dark cloud rains on me, a thunderstorm chasing me down the
    street
I'm running fast to hide from its path

Part of you we take with us, from now until the end, our limited
    time
Your spirit lives on in our lives
People hug me holding tight, I feel the warmth and love surround
I wish it was you who's embracing me

I miss you; I miss you; I miss you right now
Yeah, I miss you right now
So don't let me, don't let me, don't let me frown
I think I'm losing my friend now
I'm in bed trying to cope
We'll meet again soon I suppose
So don't let me, don't let me, don't let me frown
Don't let me frown

Death's a Doorway

(Adapted from the melody of "Save Your Tears" by The Weeknd)

So many people are living long
Prevented from dying, their death's prolonged
Technology's postponing their goodbyes
So, folks have become sicker I surmise

I don't know why they choose to suffer
They make me cry, all I can do is comfort

Are you afraid or just too scared to part?   Heb 2:15
You don't know exactly where you'll depart?   John 5:24
If you don't believe, then I'll say a prayer   Rev 20:15
You won't be alone, I'll be right there

I don't know why you won't reconsider
He's the only one who can deliver   John 14:6

I'll do my best to keep you alive
But when He calls your name . . .   Job 14:5
If you believe—death's a doorway   1 Thess 5:9–10
If you believe—death's a doorway

So, medicine's advanced, benefits outweigh
Few things reverse, but bodies still decay
We intervene and follow strict guidelines
And we can give you drugs to stop flatlines

I don't know why people fear the day   Matt 6:34
When their time is done and have to cut away
You have to choose, there's just two pathways   Matt 7:13
But when He calls your name . . .

I empathize and I advocate
I adjust the drips, I calibrate

If you believe—death's a doorway
If you believe—death's a doorway

I don't know why you won't just obey   Gal 5:13
Just surrender and He'll convey   Matt 16:24
If you believe—death's a doorway
I said if you believe—death's a doorway
If you believe—death's a doorway

Quietly Leaving

Confined to bed on Tuesday, your body pierced with pain
Last Rights delivered promptly; your last breath not long
    sustained
Your journey has commenced, your face now free of pain
So peaceful and distinguished, a grasped rosary is displayed

We comfort one another, while the kids wander the pews
Your two brothers noted absent, one last moment to bid adieu
A handful of us standing, just two dare speak any words
The church is grand, but empty; this saddens me in turn

Many more should've been present, for none have sent regrets
Family, what is it to them? They've chosen to just forget
Several think you died alone; but I know that you did not
As God was by your side; yet for the rest, He may not   Matt 28:20

It's strange without your presence, the world has changed no
    doubt
Shaded below an old oak tree, I say farewell as your body drops
You cared for us in diapers and helped us grow into men
You were always there to listen, for whatever we'd depend

You drove us where we needed; when scared, you shared your
    bed
All this without conditions, you scratched our backs upon request
Few can behave so selfless as you have done so right
You have left quite an impression that will remain with us for life

Soon a Memory

(Adapted from the melody of "In The End" by Linkin Park)

The time has come

Why can't you let me go?
There's no more time left to borrow
Time's running out, soon you'll be without
And then there'll be no doubt

All I want

Life is such a short-filled dream
In a blink of an eye, it's lost it seems
Time disappears all while we age
There's no guarantee, disengage

It's not fair

It's sad, my distant stares
Unable to close all my affairs
You watch me from across the room
Is today the day? You presume

Nothing left

I gave you everything I had
But please don't remain sad, celebrate life
As you once loved me
Unconditionally, soon a memory, as my wife

I'm not living
I'm just existing
Not my wish
Why are you so selfish?
I try to speak
But I'm too weak
Not my wish
Why are you so selfish?

I'm sure, I've started to die
You can't stop fate even if you'd try
Keep this in mind, you must live your life
To the fullest tomorrow without strife

I fought so hard   I tried so hard in spite of the ways you've been
treating me
Prolonging my pain even to the nth degree
Nothing will change but the pain that you feel
That continues to grow in your heart concealed

It's a lost cause   Things didn't turn out the way we thought
Hoping that my death won't forever haunt
You or the boys, crushing your hopes
Please face the facts and let me go

It's the end   I gave you everything I had
But please don't remain sad, celebrate life
As you once loved me
Unconditionally, soon a memory, as my wife

I'm not living
I'm just existing
Not my wish
Why are you so selfish?
I try to speak
But I'm too weak
Not my wish
Why are you so selfish?

I've put my trust in you
To decide what's best to do
But all this?
Can't you see I'm suffering through?

I've put my trust in you
But you hope for a miracle
At what cost?
Being a hostage . . . miserable

I'm not living
I'm just existing
Not my wish
Why are you so selfish?
I try to speak
But I'm too weak
Not my wish
Why are you so selfish?

Answer the Door

(Adapted from the melody of "Only The Dark" by Pet Sop Boys)

Sometimes, it must be facing your own death
That finally gets your attention; you're suddenly out of breath
Because you have denied the existence of Jesus Christ   Mark 8:38
You must make an important choice; this is the purpose of life
                                                            Matt 7:13

Although it's stark, your decision will mark
Your free will soon cast   Gal 5:13
My fundamental goal is to save your soul   John 3:16–17
Paradise unsurpassed   Luke 23:43

Please prepare, I stand at your door and continually
     knock   Rev 3:20–21
I'll wait there until you answer the door; then heaven unlocks
                                                            Rev 21

I've waited long to inquire, let your bruised heart show
There's no turning back, it's time to let your decision be known

I want to adopt, I must intercede   Eph 1:3–6
I approve of you   Prov 16:7–9
Let go. This world's temporal, My Spirit's eternal   2 Cor 4:18
I breathed life into you   Gen 2:7

Please prepare, I stand at your door and continually knock
I'll wait there until you answer the door; then heaven unlocks

How quickly your health is declining
You don't have control over this circumstance   1 Chr 29:11–12
You can't win, so please just stop fighting
You can't earn My grace; it'll be freely provided at last   Eph 2:8–9

Although it's stark, your decision will mark
Your free will soon cast
My fundamental goal is to save your soul
Paradise unsurpassed

Please prepare, I stand at your door and continually knock
I'll wait there until you answer the door; then heaven unlocks

Headstone

(Adapted from the melody of "Need You Now" by Lady Antebellum)

I read your name listed on a large stone outdoors
There are two significant dates, but what does your dash stand
    for?
What was your legacy that you left behind?
What exactly did you define?

And when your brief time here's done
Maybe someone you love will surround
I wish it could be told, wish your dash would unfold
And you're heaven-bound   2 Cor 5:8; Matt 18:18–20

And I wonder about the things you espoused
I will be around

I wish I could have spent more time just with you before
I'd do things quite differently if I could reverse this for sure
What was your legacy that you left behind?
What exactly did you define?

And when your brief time here's done
You shouldn't be stuck, return to Him, and how   Eccl 12:7
I wish it could be told, wish your dash would unfold
And you're heaven-bound

And I wonder about the things you espoused
I will be around

You fought the good fight; you did all you were called 2 Tim 4:7–8

And when your brief time here's done
Maybe someone you love will surround
I wish it could be told, wish your dash would unfold

And you're heaven-bound
And I wonder about the things you espoused

I will be around
I will be around
Certainly, I will be around

He Salutes You

(Adapted from the melody of "For Those About To Rock (We Salute You)" by AC/DC)

As day becomes night
As you take to flight

Your name has been sounded
While the rest of us begin to grieve
We are all believers   John 11:25–26
Facing our emotions as you leave

Surrender to God's design   Matt 11:28
A new normal is underway
We comfort each other just because
You're passing through a doorway   1 Thess 5:9–10

He stands at 12 o'clock; he salutes you
He stands at 12 o'clock; he salutes you

These rare moments are what defines
All that you believe is true
Hoping one day to reunite   1 Thess 4:13–18
You've set sail and are now out of view   Eccl 12:7

He stands at 12 o'clock; he salutes you
He stands at 12 o'clock; he salutes you
He stands at 12 o'clock; he salutes you
He stands at 12 o'clock; he salutes you

From one serviceman to another retired
Both of you have pulled through
No one knows your demons, can't imagine
Bound for heaven en route

He stands at 12 o'clock—admire—he salutes you
He stands at 12 o'clock; he salutes you
He stands at 12 o'clock—admire—he salutes you

Admire
He salutes you, he salutes you

He stands at 12 o'clock; he salutes you
He stands at 12 o'clock; he salutes you
He stands at 12 o'clock; he salutes you
He stands at 12 o'clock; he salutes you

To each their own, but death you can't escape   Heb 9:27
In your ascent, he salutes you
He salutes you; he salutes you, he salutes you
He salutes you in your ascent; he salutes you

Admire

Deathbed

(Adapted from the melody of "I don't wanna" by Pet Shop Boys)

"I'm not gonna; I'm not gonna; I'm not gonna; I'm not gonna"
"I'm not gonna," he shouts—outside, his eyes are glancing
He used to be so proud—leave me alone, he's demanding

Nothing enjoyed
He's getting harder to arouse
And he moans
I'm asking him to lie down

Not ready to die
He sits in his chair and refuses to comply
On others for everything he relies

"I'm not gonna," he shouts—outside, his eyes are glancing
He used to be so proud—leave me alone, he's demanding

Another daylight
His skin continues to redden
What's the fuss?
Defiance's his last expression

My last appeal
He knows exactly what that bed reveals
The end of his life now becomes so real

"I'm not gonna," he shouts—outside, his eyes are glancing
He used to be so proud—leave me alone, he's demanding

"I'm not gonna," he shouts—outside, his eyes are glancing
He used to be so proud—leave me alone, he's demanding

"I'm not gonna; I'm not gonna; I'm not gonna; I'm not gonna"

All the meds, he drifts; "It's strange," he answers
It's quiet, just us here; the process advances

Peacefully, his face goes pale quite suddenly
He's finally in God's custody   Eccl 12:7
Tears swell up with all the memories

"I'm not gonna," he shouts—outside, his eyes are glancing
He used to be so proud—leave me alone, he's demanding

"I'm not gonna; I'm not gonna; I'm not gonna; I'm not gonna"

Falling Asleep

(Adapted from the melody of "How You Remind Me" by Nickelback)

We all have a limited lifespan; there'll come a time when you'll be
    leaving   Gen 6:3
You'll know your fate before then; it all depends on what you
    believe in   Rom 10:9–11

Could this be what happens when you fall asleep?

Could this be what happens when you sleep if you're
    a Christian?   1 Thess 4:13–18
Could this be what happens when you sleep if you're a Christian?

I once had a procedure, fell into unconscious territory
I drifted even deeper, escaped to a place hidden from me

Lost sense of time; I perceived those hours were strangely
    compressed
Is this what it's like when you die? Live your life with no regrets
                                       Isa 40:31

Yeah, yeah, yeah; it's God's plan   Jer 29:11
Yeah, yeah, yeah; it's God's plan

With propofol, I lied flat; my soul and spirit had time to explore
I blinked, didn't understand; absent in the body, yet present with
    the Lord   2 Cor 5:8

Could this be what happens when you sleep if you're a Christian?
Could this be what happens when you sleep if you're a Christian?

I once had a procedure, fell into unconscious territory
I drifted even deeper, escaped to a place hidden from me

Lost sense of time; I perceived those hours were strangely
   compressed
Is this what it's like when you die? Live your life with no regrets

Yeah, yeah, yeah; it's God's plan
Yeah, yeah, yeah; it's God's plan
Yeah, yeah, yeah; it's God's plan
Yeah, yeah, yeah; it's God's plan

We all have a limited lifespan; there'll come a time when you'll be
   leaving
Could this be what happens when you fall asleep?
Could this be what happens when you sleep?
Could this be what happens when you sleep if you're a Christian?
Could this be what happens when you sleep if you're a Christian?

I once had a procedure, fell into unconscious territory
I drifted even deeper, escaped to a place hidden from me

Lost sense of time; I perceived those hours were strangely
   compressed
Is this what it's like when you die? Live your life with no regrets

Yeah, yeah; live your life with no regrets
Yeah, yeah; live your life with no regrets
Yeah, yeah; live your life with no regrets
Yeah, yeah; it's God's plan

The Kindest Words

(Adapted from the melody of "Rushing Up That Hill (A Deal with God)" by Kate Bush)

I did it covertly
I was afraid of what it would reveal
I was afraid to say hello, thought you would curse me
I was overcome by guilt, inside I was debating   2 Cor 12:9

I was afraid it would ruin me
If only you understood
My smile was a facade
But your words gave me the gift of grace—yes   1 Pet 5:10

I thought I was composed; I tried to remain still
My emotions were building; if only you understood

I spoke and you heard me
Your response came as a surprise
While she was alive, I surely helped her
Versus when she was gone, no remorse

The Bible verse I shared she loved   Heb 4:12–13
In reflection, I said I was so sorry; indeed genuinely
These were the kindest words affectionately; if only you
    understood

My smile was a facade
But your words gave me the gift of grace—yes

I thought I was composed; I tried to remain still
My emotions were building; if only you understood

It's true; indeed genuinely
These were the kindest words affectionately
I'm grateful, blame-free; I'm no longer guarding

In the future, just confront things; don't allow
No longer shameful; I'm no longer guarding
Your imagination makes it so deleterious; if only you understood

My smile was a facade
But your words gave me the gift of grace—yes
I thought I was composed; I tried to remain still
Relief blossoms

If only you understood; my smile was a facade
But your words gave me the gift of grace—yes
I thought I was composed; I tried to remain still
Relief blossoms

If only you understood
My smile was a facade
But your words gave me the gift of grace—yes

If only you understood, I tried to remain still
If only you understood, I tried to remain still

HELL

The Scariest Words

(Adapted from the melody of "Someone You Loved" by Lewis Capaldi)

The day will come when your life will end and you will awaken
Your physical life has ended; and no, you are not mistaken

You might think this is surreal
Was this disclosed?
Why didn't you listen?
You feel so exposed

It's too late to pray, too late to convey
You always took the broad road and chose the wide gate

Matt 7:13

There are no deeds, Jesus won't allow   Rev 3:20
You're standing there; "I never knew you"   Matt 7:23
What a scary sound, all your hope is lost
"Depart from me who practices lawlessness"; you've been judged

Matt 7:23

"For God so loved the world, that he gave his only Son, that
   whoever   John 3:16[1]
believes in him should not perish" but rather be saved forever

Please don't ever forgo, it's been revealed
A personal relationship is needed to be sealed   Rev 3:20

There's no one to blame, don't be ashamed
Time's running out for you, don't be forsaken

There are no deeds, Jesus won't allow
You're standing there; "I never knew you"
What a scary sound, all your hope is lost
"Depart from me who practices lawlessness"; you've been judged

---

1. ESV.

So why don't you instead be wise?
Don't compromise, don't let it be a surprise
Wouldn't you prefer to be crowned while God surrounds?

Isa 62:3

For there are no deeds, Jesus won't allow
You're standing there; "I never knew you"
What a scary sound, all your hope is lost
"Depart from me who practices lawlessness"; you've been judged

There are no deeds, Jesus won't allow
You're standing there; "I never knew you"
What a scary sound, all your hope is lost
"Depart from me who practices lawlessness"; you've been judged

What a scary sound, all your hope is lost
"Depart from me who practices lawlessness"; you've been judged

Infernum (Hell)

(Adapted from the melody of "Panic Room" by Au/Ra)

Welcome to your . . . welcome to your . . . welcome to your . . .
    welcome to your . . .

Much weeping, dark feeling	Matt 25:30
I've never known this place	Ps 9:17
Teeth gnashing, hope crashing	Matt 8:12
I can't believe my fate	Matt 10:28

I lived my life freely	
Not followed Christ really	Matt 10:38
Eternally lost from grace	Rev 20:15
The demons clench tightly	Mark 9:18
Escape is unlikely	Matt 25:46
I'm uncertain what awaits	2 Thess 1:9

Welcome to your infernum	
The place where you soul occupies	Rev 20:13–14
Under some, under some	
Welcome to your infernum	
It's too late to change your outcome	Ps 37:22
Or differ from, differ from	

Welcome to your infernum
Welcome to your . . . welcome to your . . . welcome to your . . .
    welcome to your . . .

Cries yearning, all's burning	Matt 13:50; Mark 9:43
Give heed to blaring sobs	
Intense hurting, constant squirming	
Banished hence from God	Jer 23:39; Num 15:30
I lived my life freely	
Not followed Christ really	
Eternally lost from grace	

The demons clench tightly
Escape is unlikely
I'm uncertain what awaits

Welcome to your infernum
The place where you soul occupies
Under some, under some
Welcome to your infernum
It's too late to change your outcome
Or differ from, differ from

Welcome to your infernum
Welcome to your . . . welcome to your . . .

I wished I paid attention
Your warnings to renounce my will
I'm a jaded prisoner
Consuming fire that's yet fulfilled   Jude 1:7

I wished I paid attention
Welcome to your . . . welcome to your . . .
Your warnings to renounce my will
Welcome to your . . . welcome to your . . .
I'm a jaded prisoner
Welcome to your . . . welcome to your . . .
Consuming fire that's yet fulfilled
Welcome to your . . . welcome to your . . .

Welcome to your infernum
The place where you soul occupies
Under some, under some
Welcome to your infernum
It's too late to change your outcome
Or differ from, differ from

Much weeping, dark feeling
I've never known this place

About the Author

Eric Zack is a born-again Christian who resorted to poetry as his preferred emotional outlet at the age of twenty years old. At that time, his dear mother died from metastatic cancer at the age of thirty-nine years old. His mother's cancer was not directly talked about in the open with him or his three younger brothers, although she was diagnosed several years before her death. He was raised in a stable middle-class home environment in a small town in the middle of the United States in the Roman Catholic faith and served as an altar boy for several years growing up. He had a difficult time processing what had happened and stepped away from his faith temporarily as he coped and adjusted with this "new normal." Fortunately, he soon returned to his faith with a renewed passion to develop a closer relationship with his Savior Jesus Christ while trying to better understand life, suffering, loss, and healing. His personal mission statement and professional goals have been to "make a difference and help others" because he was not able to do so for his mother.

Since a young age, Eric has generally possessed an introvert personality type and has often kept his thoughts and feelings private for the most part until now. He is also an experienced and expert oncology nurse and nursing college professor in response to his mom's death, which occurred during his third year of college. Today, he is married and has four adult children, none of whom have ever met his mother. Eric's poetry has dealt with most aspects of living life and covers many different, unique topics that most human beings will experience. More recently, he has been driven to write about many aspects of his maturing Christian faith. He noted a significant gap in the literature in regard to Christian poetry that is supported by the Holy Bible and the many truths that the Holy Bible shares. As a result, he wanted to publish his poetry collections to share with whomever is interested in learning more about these topics, whomever enjoys reading and meditating on various Bible verses, and whomever enjoys poetry in general. He felt it a priority at this time in his life to pursue publishing these five volumes to help others in their spiritual journeys given today's serious crises and waning timeline.

His other poetry collections that are not directly related to Christianity may be published at a future date. Eric's poetry style is typically rhythmic and rhyming in nature with repeated chorus lines (almost like a song) to support certain important aspects worth stressing. Up to this point, his poems have been hidden from all and considered amateur (never shared or published before). This has been his "quiet" passion for over thirty years now; and he hopes that some good may come out of him sharing these authentic, cherished poems that are very personal and private in nature. He sincerely believes that the Holy Spirit has coauthored most of these, using him as a vessel to reach others who are in desperate need of answers and/or support.

Thank you for allowing small pieces of me and my life's insight into your reality and life. And may Jesus Christ have all the power, praise, and glory for doing so. And may God continue to bless you and your loved ones as you seek to get closer and closer to Him. In Christ Jesus, Eric.